CAREY SALERNO

Shelter

Alice James Books
FARMINGTON, MAINE

10 9 8 7 6 5 4 3 2 1

Alice James Books are published by Alice James Poetry Cooperative, Inc., an affiliate of the University of Maine at Farmington.

ALICE JAMES BOOKS
238 MAIN STREET
FARMINGTON, ME 04938

www.alicejamesbooks.org

LIBRARY OF CONGRESS CATALOGING-IN-PUBLICATION DATA
Salerno, Carey.
Shelter / Carey Salerno.
   p.   cm.
Poems.
ISBN-13: 978-1-882295-72-2
ISBN-10: 1-882295-72-2
I. Title.
PS3619.A4348S54 2009
811'.6--dc22   2008038273

Alice James Books gratefully acknowledges support from the University of Maine at Farmington and the National Endowment for the Arts. 🌱

Cover art: Gavin Will, "2dogs"
© 2005 by Gavin Will, www.gavinwill.me.uk
Courtesy of the artist

SHELTER

FOR DAN

AND FOR MY GRANDFATHER

Acknowledgments

"Asylum" received Honorable Mention for the *Rattle* 2006 Poetry Prize and appeared (in an earlier version) in *Rattle*, Winter 2006.

Gratitude to my family, the editors, fellow Alices, and staff of AJB; and to my Henniker mentors, friends, and classmates all of whom have graced me with tremendous inspiration and guidance.

Contents

Fledgling 3
White Wolf 4
A Surrender 5
Instead of a Shotgun 7
Euthanasia (e-room) 8
Lessons 9
Shelter 12
Sunday Morning 13
Skipping Stones 14
The Rabies Treatment 15
Entre Chien et Loup 17
Yellow Labrador 18
Certification 19
Shewolves 20

Burnout 23
A Business of Killing 24
Sanctuary 26
Black Chow Chow 27
Cleaning the Storage Freezer 28
Petunia 29
Thanksgiving 30
Dinner Date 31
Communion 32

On Toes, on Ketamine   35
Martyrdom   36
Boss   37
Neuter   38
Omertà   39
Narthex   40
Stray   41
Asylum   42

Bars Like Ribbons   47
Ozzie and Harriet   49
Puppy   50
Permanent Address   51
They Set a Date by Averaging the Number   53
Lilac Thieves   54
Opossum   55
Beach Masque with Dog   57
Stillbirth with Beagle and Kennel Staff   58
Wedding Invitation   59
Ritual   60
Unraveling   61
Much Like a Mother   62
Afterlife   63
The Unlit Seam   64

FLEDGLING

Tina fastens the needle,
barrel blue to 1cc.

A dose we divide for seven
kittens. I pinch one by the scruff.

Hind legs scrunch to haunches;
he hangs, a sack of bones.

We turn from the purple carrier,
backs to the mother, guttural moan.

Kittens, velvet skeletons, wither
in my hands, cumbersome skulls

drooping without muscle. Their tongues
strain to brush ashen noses—

then slacken, knock against loose jaws
unmasking porcelain, pushpin teeth.

Tina rustles out a garbage bag, inhales
sterile plastic. I drop in kittens, some not

yet dead, cull more juice and hoist mother.
I wrap fingers like tape on legs, stretching

her urine-damp body. She doesn't fight
as Tina draws closer, knowing

the angle at which to pierce a heart.

WHITE WOLF

There are dogs going mad after a few
days in kennel rows. Rottweilers

mostly, we give them three days tops
until restless kennel legs

jump them in circles, barge
torsos at rusted pen doors. Their anemic lips

snarl at offers to play outside
and we say *time up*—fearing wet jaws.

She's the same and we name her Suisse, purebred
Blanc Berger, white and striking, unspayed. Snow

ushers her in because she isn't good
with children, has a slight food aggression problem,

though we hold her for breed's rescue. I chaperone
her in our courtyard and she runs me

like a slave, growling when I escort her indoors.
If other dogs are brought to play, a flash of teeth.

The diva dog won't let me pet or touch her
bristled coat when I slip the braided

blue lead onto her neck,
noticing as she prances back to her cell

the gleam of her yellow eye, the way
wet soil rises up ivory legs.

A SURRENDER

Husband and wife twinned in red-checked
flannel slam through double-glass doors,

aborting sodden cardboard
onto ceramic floor.

A wilting Cocker Spaniel
makes unholy music inside.

Husband nudges it toward the counter
with caramel Caterpillar boots,

Found it on a roadside,
diesel truck pitching its body.

Somehow still breathing,
gash spilling the underbelly.

The salmon-faced couple folds
hands in front of reception,

she stroking her fat
thumb back and forth.

Too poor for a veterinarian,
they want to surrender him, adopt

when he's well, sewn flesh
and mortared bone.

His blood sweats through the cardboard,
pools the unswept floor. We hoist

and he plummets straight through.
She collapses to her knees crying *Dios mio,*

rocking the dog. He's bleeding out
and she rocks him though she's crushing

and he winces, soaks her cotton shirt.
Not knowing what to do,

having no release signatures,
we stand and act official. Listen

for cars blowing past on black highway.

INSTEAD OF A SHOTGUN

he is tied to our silver ten-foot gate
with straw twine,

neck rubbed raw
trying to break loose.

Unaddressed note
threading the lock latch,

Please find home.
The dog shimmies

wet chocolate coat,
twists his head when I untie him.

He searches the long dirt
driveway—no blue pickup,

rusted-out cab he can ride in.
I tug the slip knot lead,

steer him to the shelter,
painted iron door

slams behind us.
On his identity card:

hold for seven days

EUTHANASIA (E-ROOM)

Standing in the dank laundry room,
I scrape shit from cotton blankets,

cram one after another into the washer.
Translucent blue ribbons

downspiral over pilled bedclothes.
My arms crave sleep, sting and prick.

As I wrap ivory sheets, clouds swell—
the e-room speeds to bury me, my name

summoned over the PA.
I reach into the marigold dryer,

draw a quilt and begin folding.
The dogs rush around me, ebony nails

scarring enameled floor. The shelter
darkens, warhorse winter.

We speak with eyes.

LESSONS

i

In afternoon sunlight, on the Harborfront Mall roof,
we got our first lesson on dying.

We stood in a circle, a group of boys and girls;
the axis, a broken-winged sparrow.

It wobbled, keeled on its face. After staring a while,
one lanky boy argued, *It can't fly again.*

He told us girls to turn away our pretty faces.
In my peripheral, skirt hems flapped and soared,

skinny wrists came down to stifle
movement, and I witnessed the same boy

take up the battered bird in one red, sweaty hand. The others
bowed, half-panting for a glimpse of panty.

                    This is mercy: when the boy
flung the chirping clump of feathers like a baseball

against a brick wall—horrific curiosity.
Two smacks. The wall; hot roof we stood on.

I never imagined how it would
sound out death, how the second snap

a sort of echo and all the girls
whirled around with skirts in tight fists, gasped—

ii

Wanting him to take
over me, speak for me,

seize the old Daschund
by the forearm and say,

I'm ready.
He does.

Takes patience— pulling
down the plunger,

measuring cobalt poison. He marks
a page in the black book, falls

onto his knees, onto white
floor, removing

the kelly green collar as if
unlatching this

hairy throat, tossing tags which sing
like bullets against stripped

metal and thread, the already
heaped instruments

posing on a bed of loose hair.
The boy, too, holds the dog, now nameless.

One arm around the red body.
The other, thumb rolling

back on forearm, clamps
a throbbing vein.

How can I say now, *It wasn't I.*
Not I who didn't

cry out after the dog's eyes
glassed over, cringe when he showed

how to test for death, stabbing
the poor heart.

Its slurring beat bobbed the syringe.
Who was I to hear over

and over on the mall roof,
It can't fly again, and believe it?

SHELTER

In the snow, I crawl out,

claw charred earth

    —like tundra—

but can't get at the heart
before it vanishes.

And the dogs too.

They sniff and howl

for shelter

    all night.

SUNDAY MORNING

The dogs rouse in frenzy.

Off-key choir when I come in,
Black Lab on my lead.

We track wet spruce paint
cedar soil
distant air along chain link pews.

The dogs bow,
bony haunches hooked to air.

Worshipping.

SKIPPING STONES

It isn't death that brings us here.
Today, it's a love story

in the stone euthanasia room.
Kennel rules disintegrate, because today I'll drive you

home in my white Audi.
You'll jump over the seat onto my back

and howl and drool and snivel, but not
run your term in the e-room where

even the open door begins some ending.
Instead we lick the rules dusting our lips,

roll in the rule piles heaped on white floor.
I gather them up like skipping

stones in my blue scrub pants pocket
to carry to Lake Michigan over golden dunes.

There I whip the weights into that deep emerald,
watch you tear down the vacant beach.

THE RABIES TREATMENT

By the time we were all through,
every tool was laid out on the table.

Our arms so weak, we dropped all the papers;
thumping hearts wild to escape our chests.

But it was over and the body rolled
in a bundle tied up, slumped next to us.

For a long while, we gaped at the head
upside down on the table next to a line of dull tools.

We had scissored it off, trying each blade
finally breaking the bone with hedge cutters.

The head so still—even when I perched
its little neck on my knee,

coming undone, being sawed, twisted, vised
between two dull blades, the head didn't bulge an eye.

And we, sweaty-fingered, remarked how hard it was,
how thick the neck skin, how

there was hardly any blood, the table kept so clean
and the tools, too; none finished the job

entirely. We pulled with our hands. Yours on the body,
mine on the head. We yanked apart the tiny raccoon.

How it felt finally to break it, and how we each half-expected
the coon to come alive, hiss and claw its way free.

The tools we sluiced, head in a box,
headless body dumped behind the shelter

in a rusty casket. The open neck.
Our hands already washed.

ENTRE CHIEN ET LOUP

Another morning when I open
my eyes, drive beneath an unstitching

blanket of saffron trees up to the shelter
driveway. I step from seat to soaked

pavement, leaves swirling
beneath my car door, read the notice soliciting

kitten food and realize it's my day off.
But I must have thought I was coming home;

here when my eyes opened, blue
morning under the cover of maple shadow.

And what can I say now that I am here
and can use this day for all the errands

I need to run? To take my dog to Hoffmaster,
let her run the smooth beach, bark at waves.

I will spend it drifting, watch others pretend on TV.
Pretend, too, my head isn't wrapped in this heavy

coat, shelter, churning wind in its backyard.
I press my face against cold fence and scream.

YELLOW LABRADOR

His body is rough
diamonds stuck to my hand.

I clasp braided links, steel
fence between us,

lower my chin and he comes forth.

Unlit air pouring on his shining
body, crown I'm too small for.

A golden blanket
that someone yanks

ripples over the sky—
how it drops from the edge of earth

silently.
And then gone.

CERTIFICATION

She's saying over and over *I feel foolish*,
paces adumbral hallway cupping

syringe. Eyes out of focus, *can't concentrate.*
Watched, observed, *so what*

if I'm not confirmed, but the veterinarian
pressures her to give the leg another try,

shave a bit of tabby fur, pump the forearm
a little harder this time, careful with the needle,

not too deep. The drugged cat's ears
press the skull. She cannot miss its vein, focusing

on the twenty-five cent raise. Wasn't that enough
to lean over and stab the heart, humor the vet's

sensitivity? Compassion: the slabbed certificate
on the wall reads so. In the name

of all holies she, he, anyone will-
ing to work for minimum wage may kill.

SHEWOLVES

You try to storytell how the wolf
trapped you, but something stops this noise—

mind singing flats. To the shelter director,
petting Rat Terrier in her ample lap, unable

to explain. As if the wolf having you backed
atop a freezer full of husk and bone

weren't enough to say she had you
cornered in the e-room, pasted to cinder

blocks, sweating. You say the wolf knew
you were to kill her, told how

she lifted each terrible leg—but the director
is hushed and expressionless, rhythmically

smearing her palm over the dog's back.
And now upon waking

yellow eyes knock fiercely at your breast.

BURNOUT

Started putting things in numbers: dogs, cats,
rabbits, pigeons, snakes become scattered,

inconstant dots on the director's fiscal chart.
Especially in summer—there are enough

incoming I suggest naming animals
by number. It's too much to have to learn

new assignments each Sunday. One: liver-spot
Dalmatian balancing on top of his pen,

wobbles on the brown metal bar. Toe to toe,
all four brown-speckled legs in a line. He must

have climbed the chains link by link. By attempting
this escape, he triggers the shelter alarm.

Kennel staff phoned at three A.M.
We rush in, follow a red-peppered trail

to the penumbra, corner near leaded
glass door, One cowering. He tongues foot and foreleg.

Some swaying plant spills on the white
floor, some whiskers, pink skin caught in chain clasps.

Boss says *put him down,* and so we stay,
unslept, unshowered and leave the shelter that evening—

driving iced boulevards home to our cottages, apartments,
the inedible, solitary dinner.

A BUSINESS OF KILLING

I lay my forefinger along his vein like a splint,
needing a fixed line from the tissue.

In my other hand, twist a syringe, bevel up.
Press it down into the Weimaraner's

silvery skin. A tiny string of blood
leaks into the loaded cylinder.

*

I am at war with his leg. The bayonet syringe
hell-bent on ending his life with a single, fatal prick.

I crave swift assassination, have learned
to aim with eyes closed,

when to uncloak, see the animal frozen on white
ground, but it hardly ever goes this way.

*

My hands cup. The dog's head smashes
them over and over. Our bones

make loud snaps that echo. He gallops
on his side, desperate, legs uncoordinated,

front two mangled, pouring
murky blood that smells of sweet copper.

*

As his body chokes, labors to extinguish
air, I look up through graph windows, pretend

his panging bays have ceased. When he is dead
strings of light pierce the glass

above me. Shadows like spilled black
beads tear over walls.

SANCTUARY

I come to see you about your pregnancy,
find you locked in the e-room.

It's quiet here, you sigh; *listen to the seconds ticking.*
You're right to come here,

room we enter only with a key.
The dead surround us.

You crouch, press your belly,
other hand brushing white floor.

For those voiceless dead we scribe a book of names.

There is no denouement. Say it isn't death
which brings us here,

that knocks at you outside this door—

BLACK CHOW CHOW

In the dead of August, a black dog
haunts the arid greenhouses behind our shelter,

salivating and frightening gardeners
(maybe it's rabid).

The only guy working at the shelter and I
are sent to track and capture this escape artist Chow Chow.

Our arms are poles with nooses on the end.
We barrel over the lawn practicing, devouring fresh air.

The heavy poles make us lumber
like men with rifles, charging in battle.

We can't catch her, though I love to watch her get away,
chase her into deciduous jungle.

It's like wading in the community pool
with school friends, playing Marco Polo,

and me, clumsily grappling the water
for a foot or hand, *fish out of water*.

I'd peek from eyelids. When close enough
to touch skin, back away. Now just for a moment

playing, wanting to be *it*.

CLEANING THE STORAGE FREEZER

I mark today's date, think of soft
crocus that broke from cedar
soil and today is wilting,
pollen like orange sand in silk coves;
begin a catalogue of names.

Yesterday, I stood in the great storage
freezer I'd dragged past the roof shade
from shelter to gravel drive.

With brush and hose, some laundry
detergent in a ten-gallon bucket,
I scrubbed the sides white,
melted crystalline blood from corners,

drained and repeated—never wanting the job to end,
pushed and pushed the wooden handle,
heaving the brush forward, ripping it back.
So proud that I did it,

the others saw me
standing in filth, waist-high
where all the bodies were stacked
even before I was hired in.
Ash and wind burning my wet hands.

PETUNIA

She's laid out
under the table
Sunday morning,

blood caking her leg,
smeared on the floor.

Chores today
are supposed to be a cinch:
feed the dogs, cats, leave.

From the shelf,
grab a box of garbage bags,
unravel white line, shake it out.

Her legs are wet birch
that smoke out the fire.
Body refusing to bend.

THANKSGIVING

On the gray farmhouse porch,
I slouch in dim morning.

Darkness pours from cracked windows,
filmy, onto the hairy black lawn.

      No woman—
just hordes of cats.

No one arriving until today.
We draw back in unison when the policeman

cracks the door—
All the relatives fled with the body, he says.

We're here for her cats,
toting pink and blue carriers,

but no one holds a sign for them.
Easy to scoop the fat few, cup

their fleshy bellies. Some lounge in faint
window light, lick between their toes. These cats,

that were like good children, climbed
to their owner's mouth and scoured

the body, consuming her, pawing beneath
the blue silk blouse—

not knowing they hunted her soul.

DINNER DATE

As Kelsey, you nuzzle
kibble over the bowl
lip, rooting
like a truffle pig
to plastic bottom.

Are you plowing
in pleasure or testing
for pills?
As Queenie, did
your owner hide
medicine beneath
your daily dinner?

You notice I'm watching
you eat, stop, glare.
We both acknowledge
I'm rude, intruding
on your ritual,
but I'm content.

Have you been
the same dog? The same
Queenie as Kelsey. Sassy,
particular girl. You
watch me watching
you watch me.

COMMUNION

There are moments I get
into flipping binder pages, selecting cards

from transparent slip-pockets. I pass a stack
to Boss. She reorders them in e-room

where another binder opens howling,
shrieks ballpoint black scripture.

Neatly penned identical pages catalogue
endless list of pseudonyms: Buddy, Lucy,

Gage. I soothe, drive a severe hand
along silken bodies at each failing

cry, say a name over and over—turning it
to something hard, something like bone

burning, cinder, a bird on the tongue.
I swallow this bitter sacrament like holy spirit,

hissing snake, run my finger along the pillar
of names, drag it like a stiff body down.

ON TOES, ON KETAMINE

Gray tabby vaults,
scrambles nowhere at white walls.

She flips over, collapsing
back to the e-room floor.

>   Cats don't always
>   land on their toes, though
>   on lunch break, we read of a cat's landing:

>   swift feet stalling a body plunged
>   twenty stories. Undeniable reflexes.

>   We pass the article hand to vacant hand
>   across the gray table, its content
>   a meteor or heartbeat.

White skull slapping cement.
The soft thump after is her limp body.

Didn't I laugh

when it happened? Didn't I cover my mouth
to hide its fullness, the wide smile?

MARTYRDOM

I cover their eyes. For over a month,
doing it all, Molly painting kennels.
The way my body molds to glass

when she hands me the keys.
I'm eager to run the show, keep e-room secrets,
offer Molly's steel eyes to kennel staff at lunch time,

no answer for bloody shoes and scrubs.
Molly paints and repaints because office staff
hates the color. *All that paint, what a waste.*

I'm keeping keys overnight. Stay summer evenings
tithing dark to dark in the white
vault to dredge our unholy sepulcher.

When kennel staff quit the shelter, office
staff call it "compassion fatigue." An abstraction
taking hold of the body. In the beginning, I wouldn't understand.

Now witness to coffinless bodies, their chronic parading
to my steel door. I'm obese with mercy
and see Molly running the brush for darker-than-winter days,

color returning to her face. I watch the white stroke.
Bristles line over inundating cinderblock.

BOSS

for Herb Scott

Boss's husband Joel gets you high—
Come out back for a smoke.
You're both a rearing team for the dogs
today, four hours to clean down
the rows; why not? You forget
it makes you paranoid, irresponsible,
awkward in the meeting with
the shelter director when she asks
about the cat you let loose from animal
control, *Why didn't you chase it?* The Shar Pei
you dueled in hazy garage, how many
food bags you counted during yesterday's
rainstorm. And *how is your adopted dog, Kelsey?*
Why is she always at the shelter? Director really
wants to know who you think you are.
Don't be afraid. Leave the hall vacant when
Joel says *time to party.* It's okay
cuz his wife is Boss, cool Boss, party Boss, don't-
give-a-shit-about-it Boss. And tomorrow,
you'll be disinfecting cat cages alone, Boss
getting a divorce, and the director asking to know
more about your life, *why so unclean.*

NEUTER

Taught to tie off the pair,
twine like dental floss,
a line of wax snow raveling, the penis
purple, we're pinching circulation.
But the vessels burst, testicles bulging
in my right hand, surgical
scissors in my left hang
limply. I prepare to drop them,
remember not to impale
if I faint. I watch a scalpel pass
over skin, break open the sac
like a flower, the stones inside
bleeding out like eggs, orange suns.
I wince for the sleeping puppy,
too young even to notice his dropped
sex, an entire life neutered.
They don't miss them, Vet sighs,
whipping the dank golden beads
into our wastebasket. But I do.

OMERTÀ

Red welkin floods the pine
matted needles   black hair.

At the picnic table
we stare at our lunch
shoes specked with blood.

At counseling this morning
          how do you feel about the killing?

But
    hush
              we cannot speak this

having conjured
the answer which is no answer.

NARTHEX

You crouch over the steel drain
and watch piss stream,

lines of yellow, an array,
                    pregnant.

Say how you woke up lying
in white snow, in the down of snow

and saw the wolf come forth.
You held on by a red string

tied to her agouti foreleg.

When she drew near,
a thought of the child,

swollen coat of your womb.
You call for the doctor.

He hears,
lays the sharp tools down.

STRAY

Because he cries as she did,
mattes ingrown,
scabbing flesh,
I remember hurling my cat
down a flight of stairs,
how she twirled,
milk ribbon winding
over cerulean carpet.
My parents, stiff wardens,
mouths gaping
to see their daughter do this—
tower over the abysmal plane,
cat stunned, crouching
on all fours at bottom.
To see her wild gaze
and know what may come of it.

ASYLUM

I still hate myself for what I did, taunting feral
cats in the isolation room, a suede bite

glove. So cold, they hissed at the fog
of my breath, squeezed their bodies to kennel

back corners, yellow eyes flashing. I couldn't leave
the door open for long; some loose, tore

bags of cat food, spilt kibble, bits of shredded paper bag
littering white floor. My fingers thumping wearily

along silver bars, knowing any second one could
pounce down the ten-foot stack and maul me.

So I took a hose from the yard, dragged it as if choking
a snake, the long jade body writhing

and sticking to intolerant ice. I climbed
on top of the cages, my head at the drop-ceiling,

poking through, running water
over the floor. The cats groaned, maybe afraid.

With my thumb over the flow, I doused every
pair of eyes I could see, the entire room dripping.

Feral cats scrambled up walls, drowned claws
scraping beige paint. I managed to detain

only two with a net, but felt triumphant even so,
though the cats were soaked and later died because of it

and the cold. I believed it was their fault, that I
couldn't get near enough to dry or warm them and anyways

they were going to be destroyed, and I hated them
because they were homeless ungrateful bastards, who had

created other bastards to replace them before they got here.
Because they could look me in the eye with no shame

or request for love and it scared me, made me breathe
a heavy fog, because they couldn't help their stiff

looks, bodies proud as African lions
defending an awkward, encased pride.

And maybe I can say I was thrilled
to torture them, tease them. A leather glove guarding

my fist. They snarled and swung out long
claws, curled around my hand as if

playing. I wanted to break that spirit.

BARS LIKE RIBBONS

Her swollen body glows
like April morning grass,
black muzzle withering.
I weave red and green
towels between steel
bars like ribbons
to cradle newborns
from blindly stumbling out.
After we leave, they're born.
Next day, named nothing special.

Mother cat hasn't touched her food.
Inside cavernous towels,
I sift, unfold miniature skulls,
vertebrae, femurs. Mother cat
lies on white floor, fat purple teats splayed.
As she sprawls and licks dewclaws,
kittens shiver like awkward dogs in my hot palm.

I choose a surrogate
who's just weaned her litter.
Kittens open pasty eyes,
bob heads to inch forth, dipping
from poignant weight.
My surrogate rejects the kittens,
drops the litter over towels to floor.

Down to half, bodies clammy
like they're breaking fever.
When I refresh their pen,
mother hisses, pacing
along her pen's slotted door.

Her litter plugs nursery air
with death and afterbirth,
a metallic smell I can't clean out.

I count kittens down, lay the last
on a heating pad swathed
in blanket, a package I'm tempted
to bind with ribbon and knead—
skull to black thread tail,
kindle breathing. Kennel staff
heads shaking—*Let it go.*

At my cottage, in a shoe box,
bedside on a foot stool.
He dies while I sleep.
I know the shelter needs
to account for him,
drive his body in, log the name.
Then put down the mother.
Neurotic, murderer craving her kits,
a full family in winter.
I wipe down their kennel,
unraveling stained towels,
bouquet of spoiled breast milk,
thinking *oh god, now spring.*

OZZIE AND HARRIET

A few years after three boys shot Mrs. Darling's
class iguana, Ozzie, out of a swamp willow,
I tried to help the oldest, Jason, get his
Rottweiler mix, Scarlet, back from the animal
shelter. I didn't work there anymore, hadn't left
on the best terms, shelter director being sensitive
to criticism, and me trying to collect unemployment.

Jason's father, exhausted from performing colon
polyp extractions, drove the dog on a whim
to the shelter after finding his housekeeper snorting
coke on the kitchen counter. When I called,
the secretary told me Scarlet was adopted,
hung up. *Adopted* meaning dead
or adopted, depending on the day.

The newspaper story said Jason
shot Ozzie with a crossbow, the unfeathered
arrow piercing his enormous viridian tail. His friends
hurried to snatch up the tailless body, ran
to the riverbank, drowned the body in brown silt. But
the paper made no mention of Ozzie's mate, Harriet, the old
days spent playing tunes together, grunting
and bobbing their heads at Darling's biology students.

I pick Jason up from a stint in a halfway house
off Henry Street in Muskegon. He's desperate,
abandoned by his family, at my cottage
pulls out a strip of condoms and mutters *let's do it.*
I think about how the boys never found Harriet.
How between the reeds and cattails, she watched
Jason or his friends drown Ozzie. How the body
drifts down the slow, black Grand River.

PUPPY

You threw a puppy in the trash
with wet paper towels, shitty blankets,

what you swept from the narrow floor—food, hair.
The shelter's lanky volunteer found it wrapped,

crying for air, warmth, mother's teat.
How didn't you know better, they asked

when you got to work, half-drunk,
tripping on acid just a few hours before.

You said you counted all the brown rucksacked bodies.
They died a few days after you dumped the one

in the garbage. Now, not a care. Not even
for the job when the supervisor phones, *writing you up,*

and still after all the killing you do,
it doesn't matter. They all died anyway,

you say. All of them dead, anyway.

PERMANENT ADDRESS

Before the Golden has this apartment, knotted shag
carpet, city water sink, yellow fingernails prying

open fresh Pedigree, he lives on Lakeshore Drive near
Lake Michigan, but who knows whether the dog remembers

the day his owners surrendered him, moving to "the city"
which is really Grand Rapids and has houses with yards.

Who knows if he is just *too old to make the move* or not.
His new master, a retired man—seated in reception,

navigating a sea of paperwork, estimating the yearly
cost of pet maintenance—is sweet-looking and might

have good references, has one hundred dollars for a dog,
so we won't complain, though it is no shock another

purebred is headed out the door in less than a day.
They all turn over kennels the same way, snatched up mostly

by staff falling in love with the American
Eskimo, Husky, Doberman, all later becoming problem pets.

When I dogsit for my coworker, I find one choking on hash
and the Doberman has a chasing problem—

he nips the neighbor kids' ankles as they pedal
on mountain bikes in front of Boss's tiny cottage.

But her dogs aren't returned like merchandise
to the shelter, like the recent puppy with the chewing problem.

When I bring the Retriever, brushed and oiled, from his kennel
to the lobby, I think of the efficiency kitchen

doubling as dining room, living room davenport rotted
and slouching. The dog's tail sways and loops, which

we understand as happiness, and the man
and I smile, pat the dog's glossy back.

THEY SET A DATE BY AVERAGING
THE NUMBER

So on Tuesday morning, you hid from your chores.
What did you think when you saw the renderer?

He unwrapped each stiff body
from its black stretch casket, flung it effortlessly

into his grimy truck. Did you want to cry out
for the poor dogs, how you'd killed them?

Seeing their bodies frozen in fetal positions,
their space in that holding cell, fake mass grave

where you locked them shivering, waiting to die.
Your profile exposed through the stained window;

the renderer saw you, lifted his brow and smirked.
Cigarette hanging from crusted lips, he lugged

the animals from freezers to the truck bed,
smoking all his smokes and smiling, pressed a lever

and the metal slat came down and crushed the bodies.
The dead broken open. Renderer simply finished,

left torn garbage sacks to blow from the pile,
drove to where they burn.

Howls float in the snow garden, no echo.

LILAC THIEVES

Late April, lilacs choke froward air
and after dark you ford the metal threshold
into my cottage with a handful,
thick stems clumping in your fist,

hold them like an offering,
*Get over this. They smell so
second-chance.*

                    Like drawing straws,
I think, picking from your pink
hand stolen lavender blossoms.

I arrange them in a jam jar,
let go and watch a few slouch,
umbrella the oak table.

These are actions I love:
pinching horny, purple branches,
boring into their green ends, finding out where

the spirit starts coming forth.

OPOSSUM

At two A.M. I swung the car around,
an ivory '89 LeMans, two-door.
My friends packed in, fogging up windows.

I let it run near the shoulder, stepped out
to see the damage, but the opossum wasn't
on the pavement. Headlights illuminating

a pink passel of joeys, eyeless swarm.
The road empty of cars.
In boxwood crouched the needle-faced opossum,

eyes flickering from shadow. I think we
didn't say anything, though maybe
someone said, *Dude*, and we fled like ghosts at dawn.

In sleeping bags at my friend's house,
silent about the opossum, we curl
into one another in sleep. Morning,

Adam goes for breakfast, returns shaking
the cold from gray fingers,
pale sun stumbling into the kitchen.

Did you see them, we ask, wanting to hear
no or maybe yes, or maybe that
we hadn't run over the opossum,

knocked babies from her low, white-bristled pouch.
They were frozen to the blacktop.
To excuse it, I'll say we were teens,

but I swerved to hit her and afterward
the car was half-quiet, half-curious about
the small carmine hearts pulsing beneath wet tire.

BEACH MASQUE WITH DOG

Kelsey and I hike the red pine stand,
chain links, black corridor.

At the tree line, white dune.
Tide washes, rewashes.

The pines folding
over pines like a swaying,

unlocked door. Kelsey breaks the dune
slope, collides with whitecaps.

The sun rides her black back.

STILLBIRTH WITH BEAGLE AND KENNEL STAFF

No blue-collar talk, administration fuming,
disclose how the night before under skylights,

moon pouring in, her sides split, literally;
shelter director angry with us for not *knowing better*,

rushing her to Dr. Moore's for surgery.
She ballooned, couldn't walk or eat.

We weren't experts, didn't know the first thing
about a dog carrying puppies too big for her body,

reasoned she was to give birth soon,
not that her ribs were breaking. Now I wonder

why the hell we were working there, posing
as experts on sexing, breeds, compassion; certified to kill

but having no clue how to save a life.
Nothing born inside our shelter ever lived—

parvo, distemper, euthanasia, stillbirth. Even us.

WEDDING INVITATION

Whatever hell I feel about it now
will have to be okay.
I didn't show up at her wedding,

though in between her quitting and my
being fired from the shelter, we hung like friends.
Tina took me to see Jimmy Buffet, canoeing,

trusted me with her pregnancy scare.
When I was fired, I abandoned her
like everything else I knew,

drew blinds, wouldn't answer knocking.
Such shame; mistakes at the shelter, stooping
to threats in order to collect a last paycheck.

I couldn't get past this.
And though I sent an RSVP, I boozed the entire night.
Woke the next afternoon, another loser

treading the bike path home in yesterday's clothes.

RITUAL

A leaky champagne bottle in the refrigerator:
sopping the frosty pink somehow
reminds me of soaking up dog piss

from the blue carpet at my parent's house,
standing with a glob of paper towel
under my foot, the warm yellow seeping through,

dampening my bare feet. I used nearly an entire roll
just as I do for the champagne meant to celebrate
freedom from the shelter. Cold towels, pale blush

soaks through, pruning my hands. How it forces me
to clean the crumbs and caked spots
from the taken-for-granted corners of the fridge.

Now so white. Now so clean.

UNRAVELING

That we never parted ways, never
untied the last breath. I couldn't stop

cowering below the wolf. Always looked
back over my shoulder, saw the dark stalker there.

Long ivory legs rose to darkness. In sleep
she hung like hot breath over my neck,

my racing artery, bloody nails printed
the bedclothes, the stench of thick undercoat.

I come undone all over again.
Her limp tongue never left me. She knew

how we would be, dug a grave in my body.
Now we are always alone.

I fear coming close to it, dance before it
awkwardly, not wanting to stain our white ribbon,

lampblack breaking the headstone.

MUCH LIKE A MOTHER

For weeks, my mother's concern goes unnoticed.
She silently studies my bones,
the gaunt, expressionless jaw. But this dawn,
she wrenches me to her, and curling
like an infant, I settle into this embrace.
My head against the arrhythmic heart, forgiving
my life as it was birthed tearing the body.
Forgiving it now for forgetting my own blood.
She cradles my head as if she knew it to be
too heavy for the neck. Our unfastened screen
door bangs in the breezeway, the lake-
wind howling much like a mother.
We defend what we must—the spirit
piercing the body. Already it is light.

AFTERLIFE

Bodies black
and uneven bow
to one another.

Pink pale tongues
hanging. You wonder
who'd left them.

See the nooses?
Bonded to tiled gypsum—
how they

braid stale air.
The sound of ash
cracking white floor.

Your red hand twists,
locking
and unlocking the open door.

THE UNLIT SEAM

Dreaming, my body calls to go back, step
over the pane, double-glass doors into blurry
kennels, rows longer than I remember, dogs
huddled and shaking on cotton blankets, noses
prodding beneath iron gates for air.

None rise, bow, speak. No eyes blazing, but
the unlit seam where lids kiss goodnight.
How I prayed for this stillness, thanked god
for silence—how it could shatter at once,
Tina, Joshua, Molly lifting dark bodies,

dumping them over deep-freezer lips
where they'd dwell until shipped to Noah's Garden,
a crematorium, spading cinder into stock graves.
How the forsaken animals' carmine silhouettes hung
from gypsum ceiling, knocked against our brows,

and afterward, in our watered-down room,
we regained silence, the dog's or cat's eyes
blank and deep as the kismet we ushered them to.
Where we, the unquiet, rustle a garbage bag, snapping
it out to test the ear. Yes, we're still waiting

to revisit, at night, the immutable scrolls we inked,
stacked neatly on shelves, each name locked, a chain
link door. Bolted, we're praying for silence, not
to meet each other in this neighborhood, but praying
to be taken to wherever they live.

Recent Titles from Alice James Books

The Next Country, Idra Novey
Begin Anywhere, Frank Giampietro
The Usable Field, Jane Mead
King Baby, Lia Purpura
The Temple Gate Called Beautiful, David Kirby
Door to a Noisy Room, Peter Waldor
Beloved Idea, Ann Killough
The World in Place of Itself, Bill Rasmovicz
Equivocal, Julie Carr
A Thief of Strings, Donald Revell
Take What You Want, Henrietta Goodman
The Glass Age, Cole Swensen
The Case Against Happiness, Jean-Paul Pecqueur
Ruin, Cynthia Cruz
Forth A Raven, Christina Davis
The Pitch, Tom Thompson
Landscapes I & II, Lesle Lewis
Here, Bullet, Brian Turner
The Far Mosque, Kazim Ali
Gloryland, Anne Marie Macari
Polar, Dobby Gibson
Pennyweight Windows: New & Selected Poems, Donald Revell
Matadora, Sarah Gambito
In the Ghost-House Acquainted, Kevin Goodan
The Devotion Field, Claudia Keelan
Into Perfect Spheres Such Holes Are Pierced, Catherine Barnett
Goest, Cole Swensen
Night of a Thousand Blossoms, Frank X. Gaspar
Mister Goodbye Easter Island, Jon Woodward
The Devil's Garden, Adrian Matejka
The Wind, Master Cherry, the Wind, Larissa Szporluk
North True South Bright, Dan Beachy-Quick

Alice James Books has been publishing exclusively poetry since 1973. One of the few presses in the country that is run collectively, the cooperative selects manuscripts for publication through both regional and national annual competitions. New regional authors become active members of the cooperative, participating in the editorial decisions of the press. The press, which historically has placed an emphasis on publishing women poets, was named for Alice James, sister of William and Henry, whose fine journal and gift for writing went unrecognized within her lifetime.

TYPESET AND DESIGNED BY MIKE BURTON

PRINTED BY THOMSON-SHORE

ON 50% POSTCONSUMER RECYCLED PAPER

PROCESSED CHLORINE-FREE

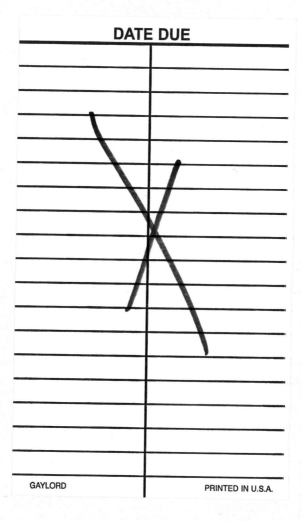

DATE DUE

GAYLORD

PRINTED IN U.S.A.